www.ReachAndyHogan.com

A SCHOOL OF TROUT

A Spirited Stringer of Fishing Poetry

by Andy Hogan

BEAR CANYON PRESS, LLC
Centerville, Utah

A SCHOOL OF TROUT
By Andy Hogan

For your copy of *A School of Trout*
visit www.bearcanyonpress.com,
write, phone or fax:

A School of Trout
1398 West Parrish Lane
Centerville, Utah 84014

phone: 801.294.3153
fax: 801.295.7920

e-mail: info@bearcanyonpress.com

Foreword

This collection of trout poetry is dedicated to my family and friends. I will always be grateful for time spent together learning of our Creator while fishing. I would especially like to thank my wife, who has been lonely many a late night as inspiration came and supportive many times early in the morning as inspiration was sought.

To True Trout Students

If you really want to know
what trout fishing's about,
Don't ask me, don't read my book,
treat yourself, get out!
Float in love on streams and lakes.
Get hooked! Become devout.
While I'll be writing poetry,
you'll be catching trout.

Introduction

This collection of fishing poetry is not just for fishers, but for lovers and friends of fishers as well. While writing the poems for this book I sent a few to a couple of Internet fishing magazines who published them on their sites. The reactions and responses that the magazines generated have been very interesting.

I received a request via e-mail from a man I have never met who asked for permission to use "The Best Kept Fishing Secret" in the eulogy of his beloved grandfather.

I received a request from a lady who was making a craft project as a Christmas gift. She thought "A Good Fight" was perfect to attach to her project.

A radio show host for an outdoors program read "At An Intersection," "Leadhead," and other poems on his program saying, "I know, I know. I'm the outdoor guy, not the poetry guy . . . but this is great stuff."

The editor of flyfishingjournal.com sent me a message stating, "There honestly has not been a single piece of negative feedback about it (the poems published on his site) while there have been many positive responses to the survey at the bottom of the page. A few quotes from the surveys: "Isn't this what fly fishing is all about?" and "I know the feeling and mixed with the disappointment is exhilaration!" and "Very enjoyable, not your run-of-the-mill fly fishing article."

With all this wonderful feedback, I began to think it was my skill at writing poems that was so attractive. So I entered several poems in a variety of poetry contests. The results? All negative. To people in the literary world these were just average, common rhyming poems. They didn't fish, so they couldn't relate to the spirit of the poems.

With these experiences behind me, I've come to the conclusion that these poems are for fishers and the people who love fishers. These are the people who "get it." If you are looking for a book of poetry that is abstract, and so deep that even a fish finder can't comprehend the depth, then this book is not for you. If you enjoy the simplicities of fishing; if you love to talk fishing with family and friends; if you treasure the memory of learning to fish with your mom, dad or grandpa; if you think about escaping from work to steal a couple of hours on the river; if you gleam with the brook and laugh on the lake . . . then you will love *A School of Trout*.

I wish you happy reading and successful fishing.

ANDY HOGAN

Contents

Chapter 1

A SCHOOL OF TROUT

A School Of Trout

A school of trout on a farm,
Safe from all danger, kept from all harm,
Nourished by pellets dropped from above,
Sheltered, protected, encouraged with love,

Encountered exciting dark shadows one day,
As veils separated to transport away.
Dumped in fresh water, some running some still,
Each found a new home with life to fulfill.

As instinct would whisper some trout would adhere,
While others struck out when a flash would appear.
When learning each danger, their eyes could not close,
Temptation, pollution surrounded each nose.

Survivors still prosper and swim in the deep,
Respected and honored, till finally they sleep.
Excitement replenished, a school begun,
Old shadows start clearing new life for the young . . .

A Good Fight

A secret stream,
A swirling lie,
A floating cast,
A favorite fly.

You hear it whiz,
You see it land,
You sense the strike,
You set your hand.

The fight begins,
The mental rush,
The four pound test,
The river's gush.

The whizzing reel,
The slippery moss,
The thrashing trout,
The sudden loss.

With one high jump,
With one great flip,
With one small splash,
With one slight slip.

You heard the jump,
You saw the flash,
You felt the slack,
You know the splash.

Another trout,
Another fly,
Another stream,
Another try.

At An Intersection

A Chev and a Ford
one blue and one red
had bumpers that spoke
and here's what they said:

"Love em and leave em's
  the best way to fish."

"Hook em and cook em
I love a trout dish!"

"To catch and release
  is truly divine!"

"Catch em and keep em
is perfectly fine."

"Don't kill all the trout!"
  the red truck coughed blue,
"Leave some for others
  so they can catch too."

"I cook what I catch!"
  the blue truck steamed red,
"The stockers plant trout
for keeping," it said.

"The thrill of a catch
  is more than a bite,
it's love of outdoors
and skill in the fight!"

"I guess you don't know
what fishing's about,
it's treating your friends
to fresh filleted trout!"

A GM towed by
right during the fight,
bashed body of purple,
clean bumper of white,

With windows fogged gray
and headlights knocked out,
but the tires still pumped
a fresh fragrance of trout.

While passing the trucks
he pleaded a wish:

"Please find my master, I want to go fish."

When I Fish Clear Rivers

I cannot claim to know
All things of God and spirit
But when I fish clear rivers
I see, I feel, I hear it.

The beauty of the wild flowers
Drawn to banks where gives
The golden glitter sunlight,
Says to my eyes, "He lives!"

The pure and living water
Rushed from spring to shore
Fills my cup and further…
I drink and thirst no more.

The rustled, leaf-drop ripples
'Neath frisky breeze and trees
Reach past my line and leader
And pull me to my knees.

Yes, God's love flows in the mountains
Through creations far and deep
Surrounding like the river
Where in the midst I reap.

What if we caught
    each time that we cast;
    still to the lake would we run?
    If all measly flicks
    lit furious wicks,
would smiles still explode in pure fun?

If no matter the place,
    the pole or the line,
    and anything worked all day,
    still would we meet
    to joke and compete
and then would we call it fair play?

Where would we go
    if all fish were the same;
    still far away would we fly?
    What if high land
    flattened like sand,
still different streams would we try?

How would we sleep
    knowing tomorrow
    had neither a challenge nor limit;
    or hearing in pain
    the splashing of rain,
still would we rise to go swim it?

What if we caught
    each time that we cast?
    In time 'twould grow to be hateful.
    So welcome some slips,
    treasure tough trips,
for such we should surely be grateful.

Learn To Laugh And Play

You boom and bellow, "Why?"
each time your frantic fly
slips snickering trout away;
or often when a crack
whips gelded leader back,
"Where's my two bucks?" you bray.
While up the wash I watch
Each manic, blinded botch,
I twinge and tug to say:

"To stay your stampede wild,
release your inner child
to lightly lead the way.
When pressure pries intense
Drag out your seventh sense;
Is pride too much to pay?
To reap with thread tied plug
Sew up the war of tug,
And learn to laugh and play."

"Patience is the key," he'd say,
"to catching many trout."
She'd entertain the kids all day
so he could cast about.

"You have to know just what they wish
and how they like to eat."
For lunch she'd pack canned tuna fish
and cold juice for the heat.

"Hard work that won't give up
is what makes us true anglers great."
Alone she'd get the camp set up,
so he could fish till late.

"Fishing is like life," he'd think,
"I'm glad luck knows my name."
"Thanks for teaching me" she'd wink,
"I'm so glad that I came."

On Common Water

Let's talk
not about differences.
Let's talk
fishing.

So you're a fisher.

Where do you go?

Really?
I fish there.
Panther Martin? (grin)

Yep, yellow body, silver blade.
The one that's so hard to find and so expensive.
I guess it's not really a secret weapon is it?

No, never heard of it.

Ninety-seven cents? Always there?
Wow!
I'll shop there next time.

Have you tried the canyon?
Yeah, fish are there.
Most people don't know,
and those who do keep quiet...

Except with friends.

A Fishing Tip

It's not the shoes,
It's not the truck,
It's not the shades,
It's not in luck.

Three elements
For catching trout;
Here's secret information:
You need the place,
You need the time,
With perfect presentation.

Where tousled trees
Strain rays of sun,
You'll see the sacred lie.
The branches low
And boulders spiked
Repel the slackers by.

The time to catch
Gigantic trout
Will seldom be the norm.
They sometimes rise
In early dawn,
And often in a storm.

The element
I must cast by
Is using the right thing.
To find that out
You have to fish
And listen to trout sing.

Chapter 2

Casting

The Last Cast

This is the last cast
for sure.
Unless I get a hit;
then I get a pair
or three or four.
Or
if I see a rise,
I have to cast out there.
Otherwise,
this is the last cast
for sure.
But
that one didn't go
just right.
So
this is the last cast
for sure.
Unless I get a hit
you know...
a pair
or three or four;
just to be sure.
Or
if I see a rise
out there...
otherwise,
this is the last cast
for sure.
But
that one didn't count
my line got tangled up.
So
I deserve one more.
Yup,
this is the last cast
for sure.
Yo!
I got a hit
that deserves two more...
Oh.
I snagged a soggy stick;
therefore,
this is the last cast
for sure.

The Cast

Too short: too scared,
too proud: too long,
too weak: too soft,
too hard: too strong.

Too fast: too tight,
too loose: too slow,
too high: too lax,
too rushed: too low.

To hear: to learn,
to reach: to grow,
to feel: to find,
to see: to know.

Casting Should Be Simple

Casting should be simple,
Just reach it back and swing.
So how did this great tangle
Mess up my launching fling?

I watched them on the TV
Where kids cast 'cross the map,
My lure flew much farther...
When my line burst with a snap.

But I won't really miss it,
It don't work anyway.
It only cost ten dollars
At that lodge up by the bay.

The guy there said, "To fish it
Cast long and slowly troll."
It always snagged the bottom
When the line passed up the hull.

I should have seen right through him;
Like those hung up fish were true,
No way could he have pulled them
From this freezing water's blue.

No animal could ever live
Where jagged ice chunks float.
I hope that dufos sees me
Or at least my capsized boat.

The last thing that he told me
With my money in his hand,
"Casting is so simple,
You shouldn't have to stand."

Casting Ever Casting

bustling beach, a trout lies

    this   waiting,
  beyond   waiting
water   for
blue   my
sky   cast
in   to
Deep   reach.

cast will find a trophy for

    this   much
  hope   effort,
lasting   a
ever   picture
lasting   to
mind,   display,
my   smiling
grips   ever
desire   smiling,
casting,   a
ever   moment
Casting   anyway.

my name rewards the

    bears   casting,
  who   casting
trout   and
till   starts
searching   the
ever   reeling
Searching   game.

Typical Fifteen Minutes On The Lake

Cast,   plop,
reel, reel, reel, reel, reel, reel, reel.

Cast,   bloop,
reel, reel, reel, reel, reel, reel, reel, reel.

Cast,   shunk,
"That one stunk!"
Reel, reel.

Cast,   dwip,
reel, reel, reel, reel, reel, reel, reel.
"Anything yet?"

"Nope, not a thing."
Schwing,   "Nice cast dude."   doop,
reel, reel, reel, reel, reel, reel, reel, reel, reel, reel, reel, reel, reel, reel,
reel, reel, reel, reel.

Cast,   dwat,
reel, reel, SET, "Game on!" reel, pull, reel, "Aaagh! It got off."
reel, reel, reel.

Cast,   dwoop,
reel, "How big was it?" reel, reel, reel, reel, reel, reel.

"Bigger than last time, but nothing huge."
Cast,   twot,
reel, reel, reel, reel, reel, reel.

"Oh."
Cast,   plop,
reel, reel, reel, reel, reel, reel, reel.

CASTING

Strawberry Bob

Each weekend's end
lands fresh trout tales.
Noon lunchtime feasts
on smoked details.

> Prepared with pride
> his lunch will carry
> a job well done,
> fresh from "The Berry."

His misty words
pour out in swirls,
bounce to his beard
and bob in curls.

> "My secret bait
> hides under seeds
> that float above
> trout swarming weeds.

Precision cranks,
rainbow, chartreuse,
at least eighteen,
or cut it loose."

> Thin wire glasses,
> warm, beaming eyes,
> convince cold ears
> he don't cast lies.

All tongues that taste
the trout he cooks,
record belief
in taste-bud books.

> From lake to lunch,
> From stream to job,
> The legend tall:
> Strawberry Bob.

CASTING

They're Rising All Around Me

They're rising all around me
As I cringe in this canoe,
I wish that I could catch one
Or maybe even two.

    The water must be boiling,
    I feel the pressing heat,
    The sun so quickly sinking
    Secures my sad defeat.

But wait, there shoots another
Three feet into the air,
Right over my mosquito
As if it wasn't there.

    Something in this fly-box
    Just simply has to work,
    I've tried at least a dozen
    Without a single jerk.

The guy in float tube yonder
Never makes a sound,
Look there, he caught another,
he's the only jerk I've found.

    The one fly that was working
    Broke off the first cast tried,
    Now all that I'm releasing
    Is ego and fat pride.

They're jumping all around me
I think I'm gonna scream,
At least I have tomorrow
To go and whip the stream.

CASTING

The Race

Dashing up this stream
in a desperate, panicked pace,
time ticks like a dream,
who started this race?

My buddy down below
sneaks to pass me by
if I don't move right now and go
he'll get the perfect lie.

Oh!

Cast and go, cast and go
I have to win this match,
Don't know why my innards cry
if I don't get that catch.

Cast and go, cast and go,
please trout, save my shame.
It won't be fun unless I've won
this frantic fishing game.

Chapter 3

Trout Farm Jigs

Wee Wiggly Wormy

Wee wiggly wormy bobs up and down,
Up stream and down stream, struggling not to drown,
Drooping on the swivel, soaking in the brook,
How does such a weathered worm stay plastered on that hook?

Oh Fiddle Fuddle!

Oh fiddle fuddle,
We fell in the puddle,
The trout flipped from the canoe;
My little boy gasped
to spill such a wave;
You can bid Sunday fishing adieu.

Mary Had A Fishing License

Mary had a fishing license,
    Which she bought in May;
And everywhere that Mary fished,
    The license with her stayed.

She took it on a camping trip,
    Along with brother Pout;
They drove and hiked the back-country
    To seek and catch big trout.

And so all week, each stream and lake,
    They fished without a care,
Until they met Park Service Man,
    Who checked each license there.

Now with the license Mary bought
    Alone, she hikes the trail.
The warden kept the one he caught,
    So brother waits in jail.

Pulling And Tugging A Lot

Pulling and tugging a lot,
I can't untangle this knot!
    The more I try,
    The more I tie;
Pulling and tugging a lot.

Lyle Frumpy

Lyle Frumpy stood by the scale,
Lyle Frumpy blabbed of his whale.
Newspaper reporters and TV crew
All believed his blubber was true.

Little Miss Whiny

Little Miss Whiny
Crouched on her hiney,
Hoping to catch a great fish;
Along marched a ranger
Who warned of the danger
Of sitting while making a wish.

Sprinkle Sprinkle Little Storm

Sprinkle sprinkle little storm
Catching trout, I'm feeling warm.
Chasing rain knocked bugs a daze,
Starting up a feeding craze,
Sprinkle sprinkle little storm
Catching trout, I'm feeling warm.

Chapter 4

Trout Therapy

Get Me To The River

Get me to the river
Away from all this heat;
My boiling brain's a quiver,
My heart burns every beat.

The autumn leaves so graphic,
Like flaring firework screams,
Streak high above hot traffic
And sizzle in crystal streams.

A whiff of interaction
With Mother Nature's fire
Clears stuffy life's distraction
And sparks my heart's desire.

Breathing deep the cool breeze,
I'll wade the hazy hush;
Frosted by the dew freeze
I'll douse this scalding rush.

So get me to the river,
A sane and simple wish;
My boiling brain's a quiver,
I need to coolly fish.

Away

Soft singing in the winding river
reels me
away.
    Away from aggression
    daring every day,
    Away from hypocrisy
    prodding me to play,
    Away from democracy
    prying me to pay,
Soft singing in the winding river
reels me
away.
    Away from repression
    roaring in the fight,
    Away from confusion
    clouding up the light,
    Away from delusion
    driving in the night,
Soft singing in the winding river
reels me
away.
    Away from depression
    dragging down my mind,
    Away from the schemers
    stocking close behind,
    Away from the screamers
    scalding in the grind,
Soft singing in the winding river
reels me
away.
    Away from congestion
    coughing in the gray,
    Away from the rushing
    raging in the clay,
    Away from the crushing
    chaos in the way,
Soft singing in the winding river
reels me
away.

I'm learning to fish in deep water
Down with the giant fellers,
Below slimy moss
Below white wind's toss
And under sharp, churning propellers.

I'm learning to fish in deep water
Down where it's dark yet clear,
Where secrets untold
Begin to unfold
And a decade swims by in a year.

I'm learning to fish in deep water
Down with the pressure intense,
Not panicked or scared
For I come prepared
With a rigger and fish-finding sense.

I'm learning to fish in deep water
Down where the sun can't char,
Where feeling the lash
And reeling the flash
Slowly soothes my heart's deepest scar.

An Angler's Busy Day At Work Defined

PUNCHING IN: Footprints through a field of glistening dew.

CONFERENCE MEETING: Creek branch water skeeters.

CRUCIAL DECISION: "Which fly?"

PRESSURE PRESENTATION: Casting around a low-hanging branch.

INQUIRING MEDIA: Spotted fawn.

SWEATING IT OUT: Sweet-smelling pine gum.

TENSE CONNECTION: Hook and knot.

BITING COMPETITION: Stinging nettle.

PICKING UP A VIRUS: Tall grass pollen burst.

PUSHY SALES REPRESENTATIVE: Cool breeze.

APPROACHING DEADLINE: Setting sun.

CONGESTED COMMUTE: Overgrown willow trail.

BLARING BILLBOARDS: Autumn maple leaves.

RINGING IN MY EARS: Chirping cricket.

GAS FILL-UP: Canned chili.

CASHED-IN PAYCHECK: Trout sizzling on the grill.

PUNCHING OUT: Dimming ambers.

I Know This Spot

i know this spot
and you
always there
with moistened eyes

see me crawling back
begging
to remember

reel me in
net me home

release me

This Here Hat's Fer Fishin'

This here hat's fer fishin';
When you see it on my head
It means that I ain't fixin'
To dangle here till dead.

My other hats hang racked
With heavy obligation,
But this here hat's contract
Is shadin' radiation.

Once I flick this mao zi on
I fly to memories spent
Sprayed with rays escapin' dawn
And splashed repellent scent.

Catchin' trout together,
We slash the twisted line
Releasin' pain forever.
Just me and hat of mine.

So though life's work keeps pilin',
And pressure squishes tears,
With this here hat I'm smilin'
While fishin out the years.

A Shiny Slimy Silver Thing

A shiny, slimy silver thing,
   so simple, clean and sleek,
   waits patiently for filling fly
   in wiggling, giggling creek.

A shiny, slimy silver thing,
   quite innocent and meek,
   sees not the therapeutic joy
   from kneeling, feeling sneak.

A shiny, slimy silver thing,
   with lightning, flashing streak,
   releases all my pent up steam
   from strife in life so bleak.

A shiny, slimy silver thing,
   so beautiful yet weak,
   reminds me of a higher place
   beyond this pond and peak.

A shiny, slimy silver thing,
   forgets me in a week,
   but lifted, I remember this:
   'tis free for me to seek.

I Love To Fish The Little Streams

I love to fish
the little streams
where oak and maple leaves
can swerve and curve
the melts of March
that raise the rolling
spring.

I love to fish
the little streams
when shadows
reach the rim
to graze in rays
and cast long days
into the setting
summer.

I love to fish
the little streams
where rainbows
rein deep blue,
but rise from lies
to take and give
a catch from fearless
fall.

I love to fish
the little streams
when snowbanks
chill or sweat.
This call though small
sings love for all
God's gifts in every
season.

TROUT THERAPY

Chapter 5

Trout Tales

Leadhead

Before my kids cast off to sleep
I lie with them in bed.
Which story will they beg tonight?
Of course they plead, "Leadhead."

The setting is a fishing pond,
Where trout are stocked and fed;
A cozy canyon close to home,
Where I oft fish with Ed.

Our time this trip strung extra short
We hadn't planned ahead.
We ran to where the creek crawls in,
The sky already red.

Just after we cast out our lines
We heard a sound ahead.
We knew it wasn't rising trout,
But falling stones instead.

We looked around and saw more rocks
Come flying overhead.
Two boys thought fun to scare our trout,
But they did not know Ed.

With one quick swipe he grabbed his line
And hooked it up with lead.
He cast it high, we watched it drop,
Then bounce off one boy's head.

The other boy started to run,
"He won't get far!" Ed said.
He reeled in quick then let it fly,
I held my breath in dread.

The boy ran fast. "I'm safe," he thought
As up the creek he fled.
Surprise to him, he too took home
A goose-egg on his head.

I hope from this, my kids will learn
The lesson of "Leadhead":
"Never throw rocks where people fish,
You might find Uncle Ed."

The Trout Master

Tell me have you ever
Had a friend like mine,
Who can catch a cunning trout
With every cast of line.
Whenever we go fish
He catches every time,
Tell me have you ever
Had a friend like mine.

His patience and persistence
Make him really good,
But something else about him
is not understood.
He seems to have a magic
That we wish we could.
Trout always bit his hook
No matter where we stood.

One time we went a hikin'
And for heaven's sake,
He made a fishing pole
From a rattlesnake.
He used its fangs for hooks
And its tongue for bait,
Then caught a five pound cutthroat
In the Great Salt Lake.

A hundred-fifty pounder
Is his biggest sack,
He snagged it in the rapids,
And with four pound slack.
We watched him land this monster
And then set him back;
A fighting, cussing steelhead
In a red kayak.

Three friends along the Weber
At our favorite place.
We cast our lines together
All at the same pace.
He said which flies were working
But to our disgrace,
The only person catching
Was the fishing ace.

One year they canceled fishing
Cause there was no rain.
He couldn't get a license,
It was all in vain.
So casting at the bathroom
Just to ease the pain,
He pulled a two-pound rainbow
From the toilet drain!

He has a lot of sayings
And philosophies,
He knows the lakes and rivers
As the trout's eye sees.
I'll share a little secret
That he once told me,
"Don't take a stream for granted,
Trout are meant to be."

Whenever all the rivers
Seem to run away,
And anglers with their shoulder shrugs
Say, "None today,"
They glance out on the river
In the sunset ray,
And see old Lynn still catching
Like he has all day.

Trout Story From Paca Mountain

One sunny August summer
While fishing Paca mountain,
I found a hidden lake
Surrounded by a fountain.

This giant, circling geyser,
Like a castle bright,
Challenged all great fishers
To a tempting fight.

For all success with trout,
As some smart anglers know,
Is getting to that spot
Where no one else can go.

Falling from the top
Of the shooting wall,
White water fell within,
The center hid from all.

Between the wall and shore
A moat's reflecting glare
Enticed me with a gleam,
And tempted with a dare.

If I could get inside
I might just find a queen.
I felt just like a knight
Armed in neoprene.

I'd packed along the tube
I used to keep afloat.
I kicked out to the gush
Through the choppy moat.

And putting on my hood,
Deciding to get wet,
I stabbed the spouting wall
With my sturdy net.

It shot me from the moat
Way up above the flow!
I parachuted down
Like a UFO.

Landing in the center
And looking all about,
I saw the lake clear full
With different kinds of trout!

I reached into my vest
And thank my swimming soul,
A faithful friend was there:
My telescopic pole.

I found fly fishing there
A surprising, catching game,
With different trout each cast,
And no two weighed the same!

A double-royal-coach,
With a rolling cast,
Would produce a brown,
A ten-pound royal blast!

A twenty size mosquito,
Tied with two-pound line,
Snagged brookies and fat rainbows,
With coloring divine.

Trout of every sort,
and some I never knew,
I reeled in that day
With every cast I threw.

Amid this time of fun
In paradise of trout,
A thought entered my mind:
"How do I get out?"

Right about that time
I thought my line got snagged,
But with a giant tug
I started being dragged!

I stuck my fins out front
And pushed down with my
knees . . .
Instead of slowing down
I rose up, like on skis!

The air from gaining speed
Filled my tube and boot,
I shot into the air,
Just like a parachute.

I held tight to my pole
While sailing through the air,
The trout sped toward the wall,
I offered up a prayer.

Right next to the blast
He whirled a great flip.
My line rolled from his mouth
And cracked me like a whip.

He spat that piercing hook
And popped my tube spittoon,
I sizzled through the gush
Like a burst balloon.

Falling in the moat
And splashing to the shore,
I filled the sky with rain,
My heart began to pour...

I never since have found
That spurting Paca lake,
Whenever I get close,
I jump up, wide awake.

Bubble Blowing Trout

I was fishing tinted windows at my favorite smoky bay,

My sinking line still reeling out the boring beaming day.

When to the beeping fish finder there flashed up on the screen,

A trout with gills a flaming bright like sparklers flaring green.

Somehow the spotlight radar beam cooled down the burning trout,

And oozing from her steaming mouth, a bubble sizzled out.

The dancing bubble jiggled up and caused a soothing start

Throughout the water world, deep in many steaming hearts.

Soon many glowing trout joined in and blew into the flue,

Small bubbles made a bubble great combining as it grew.

And on toward the mirror face the giant bubble rose,

I watched it on the little screen and scratched my itching nose.

Contentedly through stiff-necked straw I slurped red soda pop,

When breaching like a humpback whale, the bubble burst on top.

And only then I heard the sound of each harmonic note,

Come blending in a rolling wave that rocked my anchored boat.

So when the giant song had splashed along the desert shore,

I took that stolen fish finder back to the sinking store.

Story From A Fishing Derby

"I got one!" yelled East.
"Me too!" echoed West,
  but neither could reel it in.
  Either East hooked up West,
  or West snagged down East,
  so a war of the tug did begin.

                              "Let out!" challenged West.
                              "Give in" countered East,
                    but both only heard a long shout.
                            So West tugged on East,
                         while East yanked on West,
                                  till up from the bog
                                       rose a trout.

"It's all mine!" bellowed East.
"No, it's mine!" bugled West,
  but still the fish hung like a noose.
  Because West despised East,
  and East envied West,
  so neither would let the line loose.

                              "I'll let down!" whimpered West.
                                  "I give in!" equaled East,
                         but tangled the lines remain.
                              For East hides in West,
                            and West flees to East,
                    while the trout in the pond goes insane.

'Twas
the night before free fish
  and there by the lake
No one was sleeping,
   we all were awake.

          Our poles were all strung
        and ready to catch
           The trout that were feeding
       on yesterday's hatch.
           The children were playing
       Uno in tents,
           While heat from their Sterno
       melted the vents.

And Mother in the camper,
   and I in the latrine,
Had just changed the baby
   and wiped the Coleman clean.

          When out on the lake
           there arose such a splash,
        I sprang from the john
          and ran like a flash.
        The blue lake was spurting
          like Faithful the geyser,
       And large drops like cold tears fell
          As a mist soaked my visor.

   The moon on the crest
of the great gushing fountain,
   Looked like a halo
above a great mountain.
   When what through the air
from the gush should shoot out,

          But a fiery ghost
           in the form of a trout.
        With a hook in its mouth
          being led by a string
        I knew in a moment
          it was the trout king.

All trout in the lake
  rose up for the warning,
Through bubbles of mist
  he cautioned of morning:
"Now, rainbows! Now cutthroats!
  Now, brookies and lake!
Up, golden! Up, steelhead!
  Up, brown trout, awake!
Beware of all lures!
  Beware of all bait!
Let chubs nibble first!
  Be patient and wait!"

  As a fly that behind
    the green fisher goes "blast,"
  When the pole is thrust down
    a little too fast,
  So off to dark hiding
    shelters they swam;
  I knew that our dinner
    again would be Spam.
  And then in a tinkling
    a stink filled the place,
  Of oil and gasoline
    and all sorts of waste.

As I scratched my behind,
  and ran toward the campers,
Under rocks and dead trees
  the king hid used Pampers.

  Tied to the hook, in his mouth
    was a line,
  And he flipped it around
    like a magical vine.
  All kinds of pollution
    he made with this wand,
  From the mountains above
    clear down to the pond.

His tail—how it thrashed!
　　His eyes—how they stared!
His teeth were like nettle,
　　His gills how they flared!
His puckered-up mouth
　　was pierced by the hook,
And blood trickled down
　　as he trembled and shook.

　　　　I saw that the line
　　　　　　was controlling this trout
　　　　So I thought up a plan
　　　　　　to help get it out.
　　　　I reached in my vest
　　　　　　and pulled out the pliers
　　　　That I used to squeeze barbs
　　　　　　and untangle wires.

I then found the king,
　　he was carving a pine,
And I reached out my snips
　　and cut off the line.
Then grabbing the hook
　　I clipped off the end,
And as it came out
　　Things started to mend.

　　　　As I picked up the king
　　　　　　he started to cry,
　　　　He said if I kept him
　　　　　　that all trout would die.
　　　　He truly felt sorry
　　　　　　for the things he had done,
　　　　So we then made a deal
　　　　　　to keep fishing fun.

I promised that pictures
　　is all that we'd take,
He promised big trout
　　and to clean up the lake.

　　　　Then I heard him exclaim,
　　　　　　as he swam out of sight,
　　　　"Happy fishing to all,
　　　　　　And to all a good fight."

Chapter 6

Mosquitoes, Flies and Worms

The Stuff That Works

They're there all right,
you just need the right stuff.

First, you need a flexible pole of common sense
firmly attached to a sturdy reel of potential.

Next string up a solid line of knowledge
and a six-foot leader of observation.
Tie them together with the knot of experience.
If it slips, add a loop of perseverance.

Finally, your tackle box should be well stocked with good hooks.
Red faced endurance never fails.
Sparkling optimism smiles luck on windy days.
Green accuracy flies far when casting; always attach practice swivels.
Die-hard dedication is a faithful hook.
Golden-glazed wisdom attracts great catches.
White-winged patience works when all the others have stopped.

Yes, there's a high price to be paid,
but trophies of success are only caught by
fishers who have the stuff that works.

Mosquitoes, Flies and
Worms

An Observation

One observer, observing two fishy fishers,
once fished for fresh fillet of trout.

The two fishy fishers flung feisty corn
for which catchy carp found fetching fun.

Through shiny shades the observer observed the fishy
fishers' freezing fish catching cold in clammy coolers.

The big boiling sun shone brightly, frying the
fishy fishers and baking the freezing fish.

Predictably, as the prepared observer observed
a tactful trout pacing toward a tall tree,

The fishy fishers found fagots
from which they fetched a flickering fire.

The observer released the tactful trout
and humming happily, headed home.

The fishy fishers fought over frozen anchovies
while milking mosquitoes feasted on fickle fiber.

Mosquito Flies

Szzzz,
mosquito flies.

Split
worm in two.

Silence,
mosquito lands.

Slide
hook in worm.

SHAAGH!
mosquito bites.

Splash.
Dropped worm sinks.

Szzzz,
mosquito flies.

Split
wind and stream.

Silence,
mosquito lands.

Slide
the current's edge.

SHAAGH!
Trout bites.

Splash,
releasing net recoils.

Szzzz,
mosquito flies.

Catch And Release

A disturbance.

She danced on the surface
where none can rise above
with red-tipped wings
softly tempting,
enticing.

An impulse.

Her piercing kiss
yanked and tugged
my world
away.

A fight.

In reeling pain
I raved to return,
but panicked pulls
were her play joy.

Release.

A scarred and loving limb
reached down from high
above the surface to clip
the bloody wings
and set me free.

Green

To a literary order of libidos
and feral femininity:
a pen where beauty,
art and meaning
were defined by the size of
pencils,
There came a child
who spoke,

"Once there was a boy named Ed.
Who liked to stay in bed.
He had a nice brother named Andy.
He liked to go fishing.
Ed liked to go too.
Andy was a good brother,
and they lived happily ever after."

As they slaughtered his pearls
in squealing intellectual shun,
the cheerful lad,
their stuffed sensual cravings
far from his innocence,
observed.
Then laughing turned.
He took good brother
fishing.

The Devil Is A Fisherman

The devil is a fisherman
who knows each lake and brook
And every fish whose fins go swish
has smelled his tempting hook.

A maniac possessed with rage,
he fishes day and night
with bait he digs, with lures and jigs,
whatever fish will bite.

And even when professionals
spook skunks in well-fished lies,
the cunning trout flip up and out
to bite his scented flies.

The devil is a fisherman
whose filed hooks will snag
like thorny rose to nibbling nose
to grab, to play, to drag.

His buzzard eye means death to fish,
he'll seldom miss a kill.
For flaxened test leads to his nest
where talons pierce each gill.

Once strung upon his choking chain
The flopping fish soon tire.
Till dragged out death reaps wailing flesh
inside a roaring fire.

The Ultimate Secret Fly Revealed

The ultimate secret fly
is about to be revealed, it's . . .

Shhh.

The fly that catches
when nothing else is working, it's . . .

Shhh.

The fly that is known, owned and tied,
only by the stream's oldest angler, it's . . .

Shhh.

The secret promised to be revealed,
only on his death bed when he
could fish no more, it's . . .

Shhh.

As he begins to float farther away
toward a new stream where licenses,
lines, limits and barbs are forgotten,
his feeble words faintly flicker
toward gaping mouthed microphones.

Shhh.

"It's . . . the fly that's in my bones,
perhaps my very soul
is called the Skeleton.
Now everybody knows."

Shhh.

With great effort, he holds the last "skeleton"
to his lips as if to kiss good-bye, when suddenly,
as fast as a striking trout he gulps down the fly.
Slowly sinking in his lie, he whispers up a final groan,
"That, dear friends was mine, you go and tie your own."

The Freezer Trout Song

Hi-ho, we are the freezer trout,
Hi-ho, the ones you won't get out,
Hi-heat, the ones you caught ten months ago,
Hi-ho, the ones you planned to eat.

Cutthroats,
      rainbows,
            brookies,
                  brown,

WILL YOU EVER TAKE US DOWN?

Hi-ho, we are the freezer trout,
Hi-ho, you never had a doubt,
Hi-hunch, you didn't think to let us go,
Hi-ho, you said we'd be your lunch.

Popsicles,
      hamburger,
            ice-cream
                  dish,

FREEZER BURNED AND SMELLS LIKE FISH!

Hi-ho, we are the freezer trout,
Hi-ho, come see what we're about,
Hi-hag, the door opens and in you throw
Hi-ho, another trout in a plastic bag.

Spinners,
      minnows,
            crawlers,
                  fly,

WASTED TROUT SHOULD BITE YOUR EYE!

Hi-ho, with other singing fish,
Hi-ho, we plead to you this wish,
Hi-hease, to fill your oversized ego,
Hi-ho, catch, take pictures, then release.

Chapter 7

Trout Visions

My Trout

I cast my line
to pass the time
all kinds of fish about.
But garbage fish
are not my wish,
The one I want is trout.

I caught goldfish
another's wish
yet set her free to pout.
The shining gold
would soon grow old,
But old means wise to trout.

With cut willows
I caught minnows
but quickly cast them out.
How easily they died
when tested and tried.
Minnows are bait for trout.

All kinds and sorts
sought out as sport
in creeks and lakes throughout.
My fish of dreams
swims hidden streams,
Skilled fishers find the trout.

So through this time
with hook and line
I show my love's devout.
I'll find that stream
make true my dream,
And bring back home my trout.

The Trout Are Rising

One
striking mouth
sends silent ripples
rolling, reaching, spreading,
until the whole
listening lake
moves.

Each
hungry rise
reduces one more
blood sucking, nose poking
pest to a shining,
silent, silver
splash.

Harmonic,
swirling sounds
sprinkle nature's song,
joining, swelling, blending,
mountains, lake, sky
with hope
together.

Catch
the feeling,
cast your line,
keep up the slack,
enjoy pure
release.

Oft times I pause to ponder,
Perhaps a tad too much,
And wonder where I'll wander
While tracking trout and such.

What circumstance will send me
To feast with famished catches
Where ripples roar the rising
Of blooming boulder hatches?

My mulling mind meanders
O'er fate's fantastic fish,
And for one mighty moment
I catch my wistful wish,

Where far from flesh and failure
I fathom Father's charm,
Then filled with life worth living
Release the trout from harm.

Just Beyond The Snowcaps

Why do regal mountains
reflected in the lake,
quiver as the beaver
spreads out a silent wake?

How do brilliant rainbows
splashed in echoed calls,
binding rock with flurry,
rise from tumbling falls?

What do pointing pine trees
sparked from cones a fry,
nourishing sharp needles,
see in blazing sky?

Why can soaring eagle
lifted, wise and free,
circling ever upward,
notice tiny me?

How does happiness
in simple victory,
reeling nature's fullness,
know true mastery?

Just beyond the snowcaps
quenching thirsting streams,
fishing in the cloudburst,
God casts golden beams.

A Desperate Fisher's Deal

My glaring stare at ceiling bare
spooked sleep without a bite.
Now fishing date will have to wait
for this eternal night.

A distant bark, then still of dark
again wades to my bed.
The glowing clock trolls out each tock
as time drags through my head.

Loud thoughts of trout keep flipping out
each time I cast a dream,
and pressure deep down low will creep
when ere I hear that stream.

Three hours or four have passed, for sure
I know the night swam through.
A clammy sneer snags in my ear,
The mocking clock strikes two.

Dear sleep, I plead, I have great need
to catch some fishing fun,
I'll make a deal, you too can reel,
I promise you can come.

Refreshed and gone with rays of dawn,
I left without a peep.
But like a net, the deal was set,
and all I caught was sleep.

Whirling Disease

Rainbows whirling
round and round, buoyant
bodies bobbing down. Spinners
rolling, reels wound; reeling, spinning,
gold not found. Spinning, twirling, turning out,
flushing, flowing rivers spout. Whirling, whirling
brought about flipping, falling, rainbow trout. Brown
trout wince with lifting eye, while rolling rainbows arc the
sky. Slowly turning in its lie sterile tiger waits to die.
Pulling, seeking knots unwound, reeling anglers
fighting sound. Toiling hearts together pound,
world rotates round and round. Turning
round the whirling black, letting
healthy rainbows back. Careful
cleaning, cautious tracks,
rainbow gold's a
living plaque.

Fishing Reflections

Water.
Waving and running
all around you,
its calls are mirrors,
its fish:
reflections.

> Darting,
> panic stricken,
> confused
> shadows.
> Hurry and look, it's you.

Blurred,
clouded,
spreading
mud.
But don't worry about it.

> Tangled,
> tight,
> stressed,
> eternal
> knots.
> Keep working on them.

Glistening,
serene,
golden
beaver pond.
Enjoy decorating the masterpiece.

> Patient,
> creeping,
> confident
> trout.
> Wisdom is catching.

If Only I Could Take 'Em Fishin

If only I could take 'em fishin
them tailgate tootin birdie guys.
The crystal water's chill would thrill em
till all they flip are fuzzy flies.

If only I could take 'em fishin
them pickle peckin politicians.
The rapid ripple's roll would pull 'em
till relished lies feed trout ambitions.

If only I could take 'em fishin
them presidents of worlds in war.
Long casts in wind would reach and teach 'em
till tight-tied leaders rise and soar.

If only I could take 'em fishin
them workin stressed out sizzle brains.
The touch of trout slime smooth would soothe 'em
till play and peace release parched pains.

If only I could take 'em fishin
them weary worn and wasted souls.
The scent of pine tree bark would spark 'em
till hearts catch fire on swirling holes.

If only I could take 'em fishin
them pulled down, pierced, lead weighted eyes.
The joy of nature's gift would lift 'em
till split shot smiles float toward soft skies.

Chapter 8

Borrowed Lines

Fished Out

What place is that where they all go,
The icy bridge with drifted snow;
To fish that spot by highway fast,
The answer why I do not know.

The lie was fruitful in the past
When pioneers went there to cast.
I often sigh while speeding by,
Some fishing holes weren't meant to last.

So many folks still go and try,
I see all kinds from worm to fly.
And all colors of power bait
Keep floating down from that old lie.

And now they're gone, the trout of late,
Catch and release was not their fate.
And fishers there still sit and wait,
And fishers there still sit and wait.

The Trout That Tom Caught

This is the trout
that Tom caught.

		Free?

This is the fly
That hooked the trout
that Tom caught.

1 size 18 mosquito: $2.00

This is the leader,
That tied to the fly
That hooked the trout
that Tom caught.

1 roll "Tip it": $10.00

This is the line,
That was tied to the leader,
That tied to the fly
That hooked the trout
that Tom caught.

1 roll fly-line: $30.00

This is the reel,
That wound the line,
That was tied to the leader,
That tied to the fly
That hooked the trout
that Tom caught.

1 fly reel: $60.00

This is the pole,
That steadied the reel,
That wound the line,
That was tied to the leader,
That tied to the fly
That hooked the trout
that Tom caught.

1 fly pole: $150.00

This is the glove,
That guided the pole,
That steadied the reel,
That wound the line,
That was tied to the leader,
That tied to the fly
That hooked the trout
that Tom caught.

1 pair neoprene gloves: $45.00

| | 1 winter parka: | $200.00 |

This is the coat,
That warmed the glove,
That guided the pole,
That steadied the reel,
That wound the line,
That was tied to the leader,
That tied to the fly
That hooked the trout
that Tom caught.

| | 1 pair neoprene waders: | $200.00 |

These are the waders,
That covered the coat,
That warmed the glove,
That guided the pole,
That steadied the reel,
That wound the line,
That was tied to the leader,
That tied to the fly
That hooked the trout
that Tom caught.

| | 1 pair waterproof shoes: | $50.00 |

These are the shoes,
That strapped to the waders,
That covered the coat,
That warmed the glove,
That guided the pole,
That steadied the reel,
That wound the line,
That was tied to the leader,
That tied to the fly
That hooked the trout
that Tom caught.

| | 3-day truck rental: | $250.00 |
| | 3 days gasoline: | $60.00 |

This is the truck,
That brought the shoes,
That strapped to the waders,
That covered the coat,
That warmed the glove,
That guided the pole,
That steadied the reel,
That wound the line,
That was tied to the leader,
That tied to the fly
That hooked the trout
that Tom caught.

This is the cabin,
That provided the truck,
That brought the shoes,
That strapped to the waders,
That covered the coat,
That warmed the glove,
That guided the pole,
That steadied the reel,
That wound the line,
That was tied to the leader,
That tied to the fly
That hooked the trout
that Tom caught.

2 nights lodging in private cabin:	$125.00
2 breakfasts in bed:	$30.00
3 days lunch & dinner:	$75.00
Snacks:	$25.00
Satellite TV charge:	$20.00
Long distance phone charge:	$30.00

This is the guide,
That runs the cabin,
That provided the truck,
That brought the shoes,
That strapped to the waders,
That covered the coat,
That warmed the glove,
That guided the pole,
That steadied the reel,
That wound the line,
That was tied to the leader,
That tied to the fly
That hooked the trout
that Tom caught.

Travel service and arrangements:	$100.00
Tip:	$25.00

This is the plane,
That met the guide,
That runs the cabin,
That provided the truck,
That brought the shoes,
That strapped to the waders,
That covered the coat,
That warmed the glove,
That guided the pole,
That steadied the reel,
That wound the line,
That was tied to the leader,
That tied to the fly
That hooked the trout
That Tom caught.

1 round trip plane ticket to Montana:	$80.00
3-day, out-of-state fishing license:	$45.00
Miscellaneous:	$100.00

This is Tom, "IT WAS WORTH IT!"

Grand Total	$1,712

Behold the trout.
It did not doubt.
No doubt some luck.
It struck.
It plotted a plan
To pull in a man.
When I reeled, it lashed;
I keeled and splashed.

All I Really Need to Know I Learned Trout Fishing

The camouflaged secrets of what I really need to know, where to cast and how to succeed, I finally caught on the scratchy trails and hidden pools of trout fishing.

During the trying process of untangling miles of looping knots, I gradually learned that the most rewarding trout is not at the dam outlet, but in the hard-to-get-at hole from the less-taken trail. Here are some clues that lead to trophy catches:

Listen to experience.
Don't brag, just catch.
Be aware of shadows.
To find trout, think like trout.
Share sinkers and stories, not secrets.
Catch and release... after snapping the picture.
Carry pliers and nail clippers.
Look up often, but watch when you step.
Breath deeply in pine forests.
Don't eat the bait you fish with.
Don't jump onto wet, mossy rocks.
Never yell, "I got one."
Rough terrain usually means better fishing.
Bigger is better, beauty is best.
If you can see trout, trout can see you.
Fly tie.
Keep up with the slack.
Always carry mosquitoes and repellent.
Family is great company.
Friends are great family.
Make friends with property owners.
Granny knots slip.
Be aware of others, fish where they didn't.
Watch for bear tracks, stinging nettle, and poison ivy.
Catching is fun.
There's more to fun than catching.
Nature is your friend, be prepared.
Keep a prayer in your heart and an eye on your strike indicator.

Chapter 9

Keepers

The Best Kept Fishing Secret

"Here son,
  will you hold this pole for me?
  I need to look at something
  over there."

"What do you want to look at?"

"Oh, nothing, just hold this OK?
  Here."

"Daddy, when are we going to catch a...
  Hey... Something's pulling...
  Daddy... Oh...
  I GOT ONE!"

"You do? Wow!
  Well, reel it in...
  Let's see!
  That's a big one!"

"Mommy, Mommy,
  look!
  I caught this big fish all by myself!"

Why Does Fishing Make Me Happy?

It's catching therapy
    to light a perfect cast,
    see the thrilling flash,
    feel the tugging lash
    and play the struggling splash.

It nets camaraderie
    to reel in fishing tales,
    cast lines of fleeting whales,
    reveal lies and trails
    and dish out worms and wails.

It weaves fresh unity
    to paddle four-man ships,
    on family fishing trips,
    to feed on fries and chips,
    as life's knot slowly slips.

It spins tranquillity
    to sit the drifting wait,
    sniff the song of bait,
    soak summer's sun till late
    and set a nibbling date.

It angles up to Deity
    to watch my little one,
    free eyes bright with fun,
    release a feeling once begun,
    when Grandpa loved to fish with son.

Brother Ed

I have a young buddy named Ed
Who has an intelligent head.
He knows lots about
How to catch trout
Like jumping out early from bed.

One day Ed tied up a fly
And told me to give it a try.
Despite all my doubt
The first cast caught a trout,
And all I could say was, "Oh my!"

With Ed there is seldom a trip
Without a hilarious slip
On a wet, mossy rock
Or off the boat by the dock,
He always wades home all a drip.

Yes, fishing with Ed's never boring.
Youth's flame in his eyes ever roaring
Remind me of life
With no stress and no strife,
He makes me laugh till I snort like loud snoring.

They Think It's The Hat

They think it's the hat.
The faded blue one
with gray brim
saturated by dark sweat
where his firm forehead
stretched the elastic neck
to a comfortable fit.

The hat that is never blown
into white-capped lakes
and blustery streams
where trout after trout
stare through dripping eyes
at the shaded smile
permanently pressed
on his thirsting lips.

The hat he always sports,
balancing a scent
of man and boy
with banners red, and gold
letters faded brown,
still proclaiming,
"BEST IN THE WEST" . . .
and yet he's never been there.

Each Parted With A Smile

Before the war of pride and time
Two sticks fought fish for fun,
And in the stream that gives and gives
A friendship struck and won.

While rainbows raved with scarlet
They burst with laughter, light,
And gold reflections warm with life
Dripped sunbeams into night.

Upon the dawn of manhood's morn
Their river met an isle,
And knowing where the water weds
Each parted with a smile.

My Trout 2

I cast my line
more wise this time
for guess what I found out?
This special stream
though still my dream,
holds many kinds of trout.

A cutthroat's red
a steelhead,
so hard to sort them out.
Golden shine bright
brookies can fight,
don't forget rainbow trout.

How slow to find
the many kinds
all swimming round about.
I want you to know
I catch and let go,
I'll only keep one trout.

Too many fools
spitting in pools
don't know what it's about.
There's work in rain
with cold and pain
to catch the greater trout.

In this long race
I'll set my pace
to walk the narrow route.
And when I do
I will pull through
I know I'll catch my trout.

Some Bread And Two Fish

Fishing all day from the bleak shore,
he reeled in his line with shame.
All the great men
pulled twenty and ten,
but he caught just two, no more.

"Just what am I among all this mass?
I'll never know glory or fame."
The simple, poor lad,
dragging and sad,
trudged up a path of green grass.

Still hanging his head, his eyes on the ground,
through thousands of people he came.
"Dear boy, grant our wish,
please give of your fish."
Startled, he looked to the sound.

"We've gathered to learn about truth and right,
but hunger has taken its claim."
The deep, whispering eyes
pleaded soft cries,
and the boy began to see light.

He gave all he had, two fish and some bread,
to the man with familiar name,
who took to the King
the food he did bring,
and gazed as five thousand were fed.

The boy ate his fill, on barley and shad,
of which he had once felt shame.
Blessed food filled and nourished,
his soul bloomed and flourished,
from giving the little he had.

KEEPERS

The Catch Of A Lifetime

With a breeze on the stream
And pink rays o'er the land
I stand on Moriah
Holding you in my hand.

The vast hours of searching,
The wade and the cast,
The fight in persuading
All drift off to the past.

I gaze at your colors
Mature and prepared
With beauty of spirit
And life ever spared.

With light slowly rising,
Now higher than pine,
I savor each moment
Knowing finally you're mine.

Grandpa's Magic Fishing Pole

Grandpa had a special pole,
much like a magic wand;
he loved to take it with us kids
to fish the sparkling pond.

One by one he'd let us try,
we'd fish with all our might;
we saw the trout come rising up
but could not get a bite.

So after we had tried our best
he'd say, "Give me a flick."
And with one cast and nineteen reels
he'd pull his magic trick.

With glowing eyes he'd gripe, "There's none,
please help me reel it in."
So then I'd sadly take the pole,
and wonder at his grin.

But when I felt a giant tug
and heard a gleaming giggle,
I knew the pole had struck again
and thrilled to reel the jiggle.

Much older now, I often gaze
at priceless photographs,
and when I see that special pole
I still can hear his laughs.

Remember Rumbling Rapids

Remember rumbling rapids,
high arcs of purple line.
Remember sunbeam rainfall
and mallards in the pine.

Remember prancing boulders,
nostalgic aspens green.
Remember reeling rainbows
with gratitude unseen.

Bubble bursting blessings,
remember father's care.
Cliffs alive and flying,
remember casting there.

Boring barren stretches,
remember fishing flings.
Anchor splashed, refreshing,
remember time's swift wings.

Teach Them To Fish

Give them a fish,
They'll eat for a day.
Teach them to fish,
This is the way.

Helping loved ones
To learn to catch trout,
Is learning of life,
And what it's about.

Catch them and keep,
I speak of true friends.
Success bows in joy,
When another's pole bends.

"And behold, all things have their likeness, and all things are created and made to bear record of me, both things which are temporal, and things which are spiritual; things which are in the heavens above, and things which are on the earth, and things which are in the earth, and things which are under the earth, both above and beneath: all things bear record of me."

Moses 6:63